Holiday Hugs

A Stockingful
of Ideas
for Making
Christmas Fun

JANE JARRELL

Illustrations by *Lila Rose Kennedy*

HARVEST HOUSE PUBLISHERS
EUGENE, OREGON 97402

Holiday Hugs

Text Copyright © 2000 by Jane C. Jarrell
Published by Harvest House Publishers
Eugene, OR 97402

Library of Congress Cataloging-in-Publication Data

Jarrell, Jane Cabaniss, 1961-
  Holiday hugs/by Jane Jarrell ; illustrations by Lila Rose Kennedy.
    p. cm.
  ISBN 0-7369-0339-9
    1. Christmas cookery. 2.Christmas decorations. 3. Handicraft. I. Kennedy, Lila Rose,
  II. Title

TX739.2.C45 J37 2000
641.5'68--dc21   00-25253

Design and production by Garborg Design Works, Minneapolis, Minnesota

Scripture quotations are from The Living Bible, Copyright © 1971 owned by assignment by Illinois Regional Bank N.A. (as trustee). Used by permission of Tyndale House Publishers, Inc., Wheaton, Illinois 60189. All rights reserved.

Printed in China.

00 01 02 03 04 05 06 07 08 09 /PP/ 10 9 8 7 6 5 4 3 2 1

Contents

Hugs for the Holidays

The things we do at Christmas are touched with a certain extravagance.
—Robert Collyer

Heart, hearth, and home all play a part in holiday celebrations. Christmas is such an amazing time of year, such a grand celebration. It is the season for us to stop and reflect upon the Savior born to give us life everlasting. If we keep in mind the original meaning of this most precious day—the hope of our

salvation—we will have a joyful cornerstone upon which to

nurture families and friends.

At Christmastime, it is easy to get caught up in the spirit

of things. Yet with all of the hoopla and holiday

cheer, it is also sometimes a challenge to

keep our focus on Jesus. So this

year, determine to

put first the story of

His birth, the carols and

hymns that offer Him praise,

and the abundant opportunities to

share His love. Once you have established your priorities, it is so

much easier to magnify the moments. When everything feels

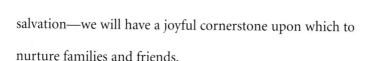

peaceful and right, you feel refreshed and inspired to deck the halls and celebrate. Christmastime is here!

This book will help you give holiday hugs to big and little hearts. You'll find dozens of quick, low-cost ways to prepare, package, and present your prayers to children and adults. Each chapter is designed to feed both heart and body. Tasty treats will satisfy the appetites and creative gifts will sustain the souls of family and friends.

Holiday Hugs is written with your shopping list—and budget—in mind. I've also taken into consideration other elements of the season—holiday

parties, long to-do lists, and last-minute
presents. You will find easy-to-follow recipes,
imaginative ideas for packaging with panache,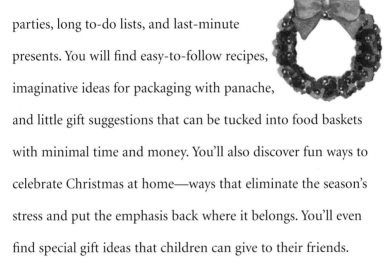
and little gift suggestions that can be tucked into food baskets
with minimal time and money. You'll also discover fun ways to
celebrate Christmas at home—ways that eliminate the season's
stress and put the emphasis back where it belongs. You'll even
find special gift ideas that children can give to their friends.

Through prayer, food, kind words, and good deeds, you'll
discover how to practice holiday hospitality and show love and
caring. Start here to create your own signature style for sharing
the Christmas spirit with those you love.

Deck the Halls

CREATING A WARM AND INVITING ENVIRONMENT FOR CELEBRATION

Address yourself to entertain them sprightly,
and let's be red with mirth.
—SHAKESPEARE

Holiday spirit comes into full bloom when you unpack the

Christmas boxes and begin to deck the halls. The bright decorations, shiny

ornaments, and fragrant greenery somehow always manage to turn an

ordinary home into an extraordinary winter wonderland. Make the time

you spend decorating for Christmas a fun family occasion which proclaims

to the world that you are ready to celebrate the season with style.

Holiday Hugs for Adults

• **Christmas Soup** — Christmas Soup, a fragrant (but not-for-eating!) concoction that boosts senses and spirits, makes a great beginning to the seasonal celebration. Cut some spruce branches into small pieces, slice some oranges and lemons, and mix these together in a small burlap bag. Sprinkle the top of the bag with cloves and cinnamon sticks. Tie the bag shut with red-and-green plaid ribbon. Include a small card with these directions:

Place contents of this bag into one quart of cold water. Bring to a boil and let simmer for 1-2 hours. (Be sure to use an old pot because it may be discolored afterwards.) This Christmas Soup will make your house smell wonderful—but be sure not to eat it! ***To reuse, just add more water and let simmer.***

Holiday Hugs for Children

• **So Long, farewell** — Purchase mini candy canes in long cellophane wrappers. Thread medium-sized bells on strips of ribbon. Tie the ribbons and bells in between each wrapped candy cane and hang them on the wall by your front door along with a pair of safety scissors. You can even cover the handles of the scissors with red and green yarn. As guests leave your home, cut off a candy cane as a little parting gift. You can do the same thing with miniature Old-Fashioned Salt Dough Ornaments (page 67). Line up the ornaments vertically and wrap with a long strip of plastic wrap. Tie a bow under each ornament.

Menu
Apple Slices Dipped in
Red Hot Apple Butter
Pumpkin Pudding
Gingersnaps with Orange-Chocolate
Filling
Hot Spiced Cider

*Recipes to Nourish
the Heart and Soul*

Red Hot Apple Butter
Makes: 3 quart jars

Ingredients
- 2 dozen medium apples, washed, peeled, cored, and quartered
- 2 quarts sweet cider
- 2 cups sugar
- 1 cup Red Hot candies
- 2 teaspoons cinnamon
- 1 teaspoon allspice
- 1/2 teaspoon ground cloves

Directions
1. Place apples and cider in a large pot. Cook until apples are tender and thickened.
2. Add sugar, spices, and Red Hots. Cook about one hour.
3. Pour into sterilized jars and seal tightly. Store in refrigerator.

Pumpkin Pudding
Serves: 8

Ingredients
- 1/2 cup butter
- 1 cup brown sugar
- 1/4 cup powdered sugar
- 1 teaspoon cinnamon
- 1 teaspoon ginger
- 1 teaspoon nutmeg
- 2 eggs, beaten
- 2 cups flour, sifted
- 1 1/2 teaspoons baking powder
- 1/4 teaspoon baking soda
- 1 1/2 teaspoons salt
- 1 15-ounce can pumpkin
- 1/2 cup sour cream

Directions
1. Cream butter, sugars, and spices until fluffy. Beat in eggs.

2. Sift in flour, baking powder, soda, and salt.
3. Add dry mixture to creamed alternately with pumpkin and sour cream.
4. Pour into a well-greased, 2-quart mold. Cover tightly.
5. Set mold in a pan of hot water so that water is halfway up the sides of the mold. Cover pan and steam pudding in continuous boiling water for 2 hours.
6. Top with cinnamon cream. Mix 1/2 cup whipped cream with 1/2 teaspoon cinnamon.

Gingersnaps with Orange-Chocolate Filling

Makes: 12 cookie sandwiches

Ingredients
2 dozen store-bought gingersnap cookies
1 dozen orange-flavored Andes candies

Directions
1. Place one dozen gingersnaps flat side up on a cookie sheet.
2. Open orange Andes candies and place on top of gingersnaps.
3. Bake in a 350 degree oven long enough to slightly melt orange candies.
4. Remove from oven and top with a second gingersnap cookie.

Packaging Panache

When transforming your home into a land of sugarplum fairies, prepare a buffet of tasty snacks. Wrap several empty boxes, large and small, and set them on a table or buffet. Serve your snacks on top of the wrapped packages. Or stack several footed cake plates on top of each other and fill plates with cookies, finger sandwiches, and other delicacies. Add some washed mint leaves and a few fresh cranberries and strawberries for brilliant Christmas color.

Traditions to Boost Your Yuletide Season

1. Plan a big Christmas shopping adventure for the day after Thanksgiving. Make it your goal to smile and laugh a lot despite the big crowds.

2. Start burning pine-scented candles on December 1.

3. Go on a sleigh ride— even if your sleigh must have wheels!

4. Make a yearly family wreath, with each family member writing down on a slip of paper something that happened during the year that they are thankful for. Add the slips of paper to the wreath.

Christmas

5. Eat every dinner at home on Christmas china, beginning on December 1.

6. Organize a neighborhood cookie exchange.

7. Plan a progressive dessert party for a Bible study, book group, neighborhood block, or other group.

8. Turn out all the lights in the house (except for the tree lights) and read Christmas stories by the tree.

9. Buy gifts for a family in need. Wrap them creatively and leave them on their doorstep or deliver them personally. You can also do this through many charity organizations.

10. Wrap 25 little surprises for a nursing home patient. On December 1, deliver a big box filled with the gifts and instructions for the person to open one each day for the 24 days before Christmas (and, of course, save the biggest gift for the 25th!).

11. Boil cinnamon sticks in apple juice for a spicy household aroma.

12. Create matching holiday T-shirts for each member of the family.

13. Buy every family member new red pajamas.

Christmas

14. Make a gingerbread house.

15. Go caroling, Dickens-style!

16. Hang jingle bells on each door handle of your home.

17. Purchase a holiday doormat.

18. Sew Christmas charms to the tops of your stockings.

19. Hang mistletoe in the hallway and entryway of your home.

20. Enclose holiday confetti in your Christmas cards.

21. Select a decorating theme for the season.

22. Address your Christmas cards the weekend after Thanksgiving.

23. Watch *White Christmas* or *It's a Wonderful Life* while you wrap gifts.

24. Keep a basket of gingerbread men wrapped in Christmas paper and ribbons by your door and offer them to guests as they leave your home.

25. Put on your favorite Christmas CDs and make holiday potpourri. Fill little cellophane bags with the potpourri and tie them onto Christmas packages.

Christmas

Tidings of Christmas Cheer

SHARING THE REASON FOR THE SEASON IN YOUR NEIGHBORHOOD

At Christmas play and make good cheer,
for Christmas comes but once a year.
—THOMAS TUSSER

Christmas gives you a perfect opportunity to reach out to your neighbors. It's easy to prepare little gifts that say, "I care," and share them with those living close by you. When you give a gift to your neighbors, you offer them an extension of your home and yourself. With schedules that seem to whirl out of control during this season, it's nice to know that someone is thinking of you. The gift of a piping hot pot of stew after a long day of trekking from mall to mall is certain to warm any neighbor's heart.

Holiday Hugs for Adults

• **Neighborhood Stew** — Prepare a huge pot of stew, divide generous portions into pretty red or green glass jars, and tie with Christmas ribbon. Deliver the stew to your neighbors as a tasty reward for finishing their Christmas shopping.

• **Yuletide Sand Art** — This dessert is a delicious accompaniment to the stew. Layer the dry ingredients for your favorite bread or cookie recipe in a transparent jar. (Dried cherries and pistachios add festive Christmas color.) Write the recipe directions on a Christmas card and tie it to the top of the jar. The ingredients for cranberry cornbread also layer nicely in a transparent jar.

Holiday Hugs for Children

• **Ginger People with Personality** — Gingerbread people decorated to match a child's interests make adorable gifts. For the future All Star, turn a ginger boy into a baseball player with hat and uniform. For your sugarplum fairy, create a ginger girl wearing a ballerina's tutu and slippers. You can buy the cookies pre-baked and add the "personality" in your kitchen.

• **Great Gumdrops** — Layer several bags of brightly colored gumdrops in a transparent sun tea jar. Cover the lid with a Christmas napkin and tie with dark green raffia. Kids will love this colorful and yummy gift.

Menu

Neighborhood Stew with Roasted
Chestnut Garnish
Cranberry Cornbread
Yuletide Sand Art
Ginger People with Personality

*Recipes to Nourish
the Heart and Soul*

Neighborhood Stew with Roasted Chestnut Garnish

Serves: 10-12

Ingredients

    3 pounds chicken, cut into cubes
    3 tablespoons vegetable oil
    1 large onion, sliced
    2 celery sticks with leaves, cut into
        small pieces
    1 can whole tomatoes
    1 can chicken broth
    1 tablespoon parsley, finely chopped
    1 teaspoon basil
    1 teaspoon salt

    3 cloves garlic
    1 pound carrots, peeled and sliced
    6 medium potatoes, peeled and
        quartered

Directions

1. Heat oil in a heavy pot. Place chicken in pot and brown. Add onion and celery, then cook until tender.
2. Add tomatoes, chicken broth, and spices. Cover and simmer approximately 1 1/2 hours, or until c hicken is very tender.
3. Add sliced carrots and cook for approximately 10 more minutes.
4. Add potatoes and cook 15-20 minutes longer, or until potatoes are tender.
5. Adjust seasonings and simmer an additional 30 minutes.

Roasted Chestnut Garnish

Ingredients
    1 cup chestnut pieces
    2 tablespoons butter

Directions
    1. Melt butter in a jelly roll pan.
    2. Spread chestnuts evenly in pan.
    3. Bake at 300 degrees for 30 minutes, stirring frequently.

Cranberry Cornbread
Serves: 8

Ingredients
    1 1/4 cups cornmeal
    3/4 cup all-purpose flour
    1 tablespoon + 1 teaspoon baking powder
    3/4 teaspoon salt
    2 tablespoons sugar
    1 cup dried cranberries
    2 eggs
    1 cup milk
    1/4 cup vegetable oil

Directions
    1. Place all ingredients except eggs, milk, and oil in a bowl and mix well.
    2. Combine eggs, milk, and oil in a separate bowl and add to dry ingredients, stirring just until moist.
    3. Spray a muffin tin with cooking spray. Spoon batter into tin, filling each cup 2/3 full. Bake at 400 degrees for 12-15 minutes.

* Layer dry ingredients with dried cranberries. Put a little note on the jar that explains how to add the other ingredients along with baking instructions.

Yuletide Sand Art

Makes: 3 dozen

Ingredients

- 1 cup vanilla chips
- 1 cup dried cranberries
- 1/2 cup red sugar
- 1/2 cup green sugar
- 2 cups flour
- 1/2 teaspoon baking powder
- 1/2 teaspoon baking soda
- 1/4 teaspoon salt

Recipient adds the following:

- 1 cup butter
- 2 eggs
- 2 teaspoons vanilla
- 1/2 teaspoon almond extract

Directions

1. Cream butter and sugars. Add dry ingredients and stir to combine.
2. Bake at 350 degrees for 10-12 minutes or until golden brown.

* Layer the first eight ingredients in a decorative jar. Write the above instructions on a Christmas card, noting what ingredients the recipient needs to add.

Packaging Panache

Dark red or green jars make perfect containers for Neighborhood Stew. Top jars with big green or red bows, raffia, or star stickers, and you have instant Yuletide gift wrap. Layer dry ingredients for Cranberry Cornbread and Yuletide Sand Art in clear jars. Top jars with red plaid bows.

Wrap Ginger People in tie boxes with wrapping paper to match each gingerbread's "personality."

Christmas...to Go

MAKING A MAILING MISSION MANAGEABLE

May Christmas blessings on thee shine,
And joy and peace be always thine.
—ANONYMOUS

It's the time of year for delivery drivers bearing brightly wrapped packages, stacks of cheery cards in the mail, and an ongoing flurry of activity at the post office. Rely on the three P's—priorities, planning, and prepaid postage—to simplify your own mailing mission. When family and friends are far away, it's necessary to plan ahead. The U.S. Postal Service's cardinal rule during this time of year is, "The earlier, the better." Establishing your own Gift Wrap Central at home, complete with supplies and Christmas music, will give you a cozy area to get your holiday wrapping and packaging done fast and with flair.

Holiday Hugs for Adults

• **Gift Wrap Central** — Help friends establish their own personal post office, too. Fill a bright red box with stamps, stickers, Christmas address labels, a red pen, and a small seasonal notebook. Sprinkle wrapped peppermint candies inside. The peppermints can be a treat for your friend to munch on while she completes her holiday mailing tasks.

Holiday Hugs for Children

• **Fun to Go** — Create a Christmas fun bag for little ones. (Be sure to give this gift early!) Fill the bag with the child's favorite things (games, puzzles, books, healthful snacks, etc.). Include instructions for the child to keep this fun bag by the door so when Christmas errands out and about take up a big part of the day, he or she will have plenty to do.

Menu
Holiday Rice Krispie Treats
Minted Brownie Bundles
Dried Fruits
Flavored Bottled Waters

Recipes to Nourish the Heart and Soul

Holiday Rice Krispie Treats
Makes: 12-14 treats

Ingredients
1 bag large marshmallows
4 tablespoons butter
1 cup chocolate morsels
1/2 cup Craisins (dried, sweetened cranberries)
6 cups Rice Krispies cereal
cooking spray

Directions
1. Place marshmallows and butter in top of a double-boiler and

melt. Stir in chocolate morsels.

2. Spray a 9 x 13-inch casserole dish with cooking spray. Place Rice Krispies and Craisins in dish and stir to combine.

3. Pour in melted marshmallow mixture and mix thoroughly.

Minted Brownie Bundles
Makes: 2 1/2 dozen

Ingredients
    1 box brownie mix
    2 boxes Junior Mints
    powdered sugar
    mini-muffin Christmas baking
        papers

Directions
1. Prepare brownie mix according to package directions.
2. Place mini-muffin Christmas baking papers in pan.
3. Fill mini-muffin papers 2/3 full with brownie mixture.
4. Press one Junior Mint into the middle of each brownie.

5. Bake according to package directions. When cool, sprinkle tops with powdered sugar.

* Cut out small squares of red and green netting. When brownies have cooled, place each one in the middle of a netting square. Pull sides up around brownie and tie with ribbon.

Packaging Panache

Purchase colorful Christmas sacks or decorate plain white sacks with Christmas stamps and paint. Fill the sacks full of holiday treats and tie closed with red and green raffia. Large, inexpensive stockings also make perfect Christmas snack bags. Pin them shut with safety pins threaded with red and green beads.

Tree Trimming Themes

It's a Beary-Merry Christmas —
Gather up stuffed bears of all
sizes and styles. Select a ribbon
color that will coordi-
nate with your
gift wrap
and decora-
tions and use it
to tie big rib-
bons around the
bears' necks. Secure a
little ornament hanger
on the back of each ribbon, and
hang the smaller bow-tied bears all
over the tree. Display the larger
bears underneath the tree
and all around the room.

Pine Cones and Holly Berries —
Collect pine cones throughout the
year. When the yuletide season
arrives, tie a plaid ribbon to the top
stem of each pine cone. Purchase
artificial holly berry greenery at a
craft shop. Remove the holly stems
and string the
greenery and
berries onto a
heavy string.
Starting at the
top, wrap the holly
berry garland all
the way down to
the bottom of the
Christmas tree. Fill in

the spaces between with the ribbon-tied pine cones.

Candy Cane Lane — Sweeten up your tree with these adorable candy cane ornaments.

Materials
    2 cups flour
    1 cup salt
    1 cup cold water

Directions
1. Stir together flour, salt, and water.
2. Knead mixture until it forms a stiff dough.
3. To add colors, take small portions of the dough and work in little dabs of paste food coloring until you reach your desired shade of red for the candy cane stripes. Color the white dough with white acrylic paint.
4. Roll equal-sized pieces of each color into ropes and twist together. Cut twisted strips to desired lengths and bend top to form a curve.
5. Dry candy canes in a 325 degree oven for 1-2 hours. Dip in paraffin to coat. Top the tree with a huge red-and-white striped bow. Leave long streamers coming from the bow to tuck and twist throughout the branches. Tie various-sized candy canes onto the tree with bright green ribbons.

Twelve Days of Christmas — Listen to the musical score of "The Twelve Days of Christmas." Decorate the tree to the classic song. Fill it up with partridges in pear trees, little drums, gold rings, turtle doves, calling birds, French hens, and more.

We Three Kings — Crowns, jewels, and more adorn this elegant tree. Use a large purple robe—one fit for a King—for a tree skirt. Decorate the tree with miniature crowns. (You can find these at craft stores.) Make a garland of stars and shiny beads to represent the star that the Wise Men followed during their journey to find and worship the baby Jesus.

Helping Hand — Mittens and more brighten up this country-style tree with bursts of color. Form Old-Fashioned Salt Dough Ornaments (see page 67) with a hand-shaped cookie cutter. After making the helping hand ornaments, paint the nails and accessorize with shiny bead "rings." Tie the decorated ornaments to the tree with color-coordinating ribbons. Place festive mittens in between the hands for even more color. This tree is great fun for young girls to decorate.

Stocking Studded — Stockings old and new, borrowed and blue, make this tree a treasure. Collect stockings from tag sales, Christmas stores, and old attics. Tie the stockings to the tree with gold cording.

Treasure Tree — Little treasure chests (available at craft stores) and petite boxes wrapped in Christmas paper are the stars of this tree. Use a glue gun to fasten ornament hangers to the treasure chests and packages. Thread sparkling beads onto a gold cord and wrap the glittery garland around the tree.

Hearts and Tarts — Use heart-shaped cookie cutters and the Candy Cane Lane recipe to make heart tart ornaments and tie them to the tree with big red and green ribbons. Cut the ornaments into heart shapes and thread several of them onto a long, holiday-patterned ribbon. Wrap the ornament garland around the tree.

Heavenly Holidays — This is an angel collector's dream tree with angels of all shapes and sizes gracing your tree's branches. Wrap star garland all around the tree and then fill in the spaces between with angels. Tuck in several shiny halos and sprinkle with gold and silver dust for a heavenly touch.

Gingerbread and the Christmas Spread

PUTTING ON THE BIG FAMILY FEAST

Oh, what a wonderful pudding!
—CHARLES DICKENS
A CHRISTMAS CAROL

Most holiday celebrations include at least one big spread with lots of food, lots of guests, and lots of fun. Major events at our home always seem to center around the menu—the planning of it, the tasting of it, the critiquing of it, and the eating of it. Traditional family recipes play a big role in our food preparation. I encourage you to do a bit of research to discover recipes that were served on your mother's holiday table, at your father's annual Christmas brunch, or at your grandmother's New Year's

Eve feast. Ring in the old with the new, or try updating an old favorite. This is the time of year for homes to smell sweet and savory, and families will appreciate a taste of history that comes along with a traditional dish.

Holiday Hugs for Adults

• **Mealtime Memories** — Make meals and snacks from the heart. The holiday season is the ideal time to establish—and rediscover—family traditions. What are Cousin Saralyn's favorite foods? What reminds Uncle Charlie of the warmth of childhood Christmases? From that secret sugar cookie recipe handed down through the generations to Great Aunt Susie's famous stuffing, menus with memories can really make a difference.

Holiday Hugs for Children

• **The Twelve Days of Christmas** — Build even more anticipation into the season by letting your children open a few Christmas presents early. Select twelve small stocking stuffers for each child. Wrap the gifts individually and place them in the children's stockings. Starting on the morning of December 13, before things get too busy, allow each child to open a stocking stuffer. This should help keep the early gift-opening itch at bay until December 24, which leaves Christmas Eve or Christmas Day to open the tempting gifts under the tree.

Menu
Sweet and Sour Meatloaf
Cranberry-Apple Chutney
Lemony Gingerbread Sandwiches
Chocolate Christmas Truffles

*Recipes to Nourish
the Heart and Soul*

Sweet and Sour Meatloaf
Serves: 6-8

Ingredients
3 slices wheat bread
1/2 cup medium yellow onion,
    peeled and roughly chopped
2 cloves garlic, peeled and chopped
1/2 cup ketchup
2 teaspoons dry mustard
1 1/2 pounds ground round
2 large eggs, beaten
2 teaspoons salt
1 teaspoon pepper
1 teaspoon Tabasco

Sauce
3 tablespoons ketchup
2 tablespoons brown sugar
2 1/2 teaspoons dried mustard

Directions
1. Preheat oven to 400 degrees. Remove crust from bread.
2. Process bread crumbs in a food processor until fine. Place bread crumbs in a large mixing bowl.
3. Add onion to food processor and process until fine. Add to bread crumbs.
4. Add garlic, ketchup, mustard, ground round, eggs, and seasonings to mixing bowl. Knead together with hands until thoroughly mixed.
5. Using your hands, form an elongated loaf. Place meatloaf on a wire rack and then on a jelly roll pan (cookie sheet with sides).
6. In a small bowl, combine the sauce and ingredients. Stir thoroughly to combine. Using a pastry brush, brush top of meatloaf with sauce.
7. Bake for about 45 minutes or until

a meat thermometer registers 160
degrees.

Cranberry-Apple Chutney
Makes: 2 cups

Ingredients
   2 cups fresh cranberries
   1 cup Granny Smith apples, peeled
      and chopped
   2/3 cup orange juice
   1/2 cup sugar
   1 teaspoon lemon rind, grated

Directions
   1. Place all ingredients in a 2-quart
      saucepan. Bring to a boil.
   2. Reduce heat to low. Cover and
      simmer until cranberries pop and
      mixture thickens slightly. Store in
      refrigerator.

Lemony Gingerbread Sandwiches
Makes: 2 dozen

Ingredients
   1 cup brown sugar
   1 cup molasses

1 cup shortening (not oil), melted
1 egg, beaten
2 teaspoons ginger
1 teaspoon cinnamon
1/2 cup hot water
1 tablespoon baking soda
pinch of salt
5 cups flour, sifted
1 jar lemon curd

Directions
   1. Mix all ingredients except flour
      together until well blended.
   2. Add flour to make a soft dough.
      Wrap and chill for several hours.
   3. Roll dough on a slightly floured
      surface and cut into Christmas
      shapes. Be sure to cut out two of
      each shape to have matching tops
      and bottoms for each cookie
      sandwich.
   4. Bake at 350
      degrees for
      10-12 min-
      utes. Cool.
   5. On flat
      sides of
      cooled cookies,

spread a teaspoon or two of lemon curd. Top with matching gingerbread cookie. Wrap each cookie with colored Christmas wrap and tie with festive ribbon.

Chocolate Christmas Truffles
Makes: 12 truffles

Ingredients
1/2 cup evaporated milk
1/4 cup powdered sugar
2 cups semi-sweet chocolate chips
2 teaspoons almond filling
1 cup red and green Jimmies

Directions
1. Combine milk and sugar in a heavy saucepan. Cook over medium heat until mixture comes to a gentle boil.
2. Remove from heat. Add chocolate chips and almond filling. Chill thoroughly.
3. Using a tablespoon, spoon out chilled chocolate mixture and roll into a ball, then roll in red and green Jimmies. Set in

paper candy cups. Chill until ready to serve.

Packaging Panache

Personality is in the paint! Just a few well-placed brushstrokes can turn inexpensive glass dessert plates into designer-look dishes. This simple project will transform your table into a tantalizing showpiece. Purchase glass plates and stencil or paint a Christmas design on them. (Look through Christmas coloring books for designs, place your chosen design underneath the plate, and paint away using only non-toxic paint!) Dry thoroughly. Add a treasured hand-written family recipe to the center of each plate and cover with green plastic wrap or holiday-patterned cellophane.

Have a "Twelve Days of Christmas" stocking-stuffer-wrap decorating day. Decorate plain white lunch bags with rubber stamps, stickers, markers, and ribbons. Use these little bags to wrap up your stocking stuffers.

Christmas Is for Children

THE WONDERFUL WORLD OF TOYLAND

It is good to be children sometimes,
And never better than at Christmas.
—CHARLES DICKENS

I love to look into a child's eyes when she enters a toy store in December. They dance with an unmistakable glow of anticipation. The excitement builds with each passing day, as she fervently hopes that some small part of that toy store will be wrapped and waiting for her to open it on Christmas. It is truly a gift to observe the glee a little one feels when Christmas has arrived. We sometimes miss out on observing that happiness when we are the one in charge of making Christmas happen in our homes. Here are some ways you can lighten someone's load and give them a chance to share a child's smiles.

Holiday Hugs for Adults

• **Instant Activities** — A ready-made sampling of fun family ideas is a welcome relief for moms and dads who have their minds (and sometimes their bodies!) running in a million different directions. Write a few of your family's favorite ideas on Christmas index cards and tuck them into a festive container of Christmas Potpourri. Your friends will look forward to some simple but enjoyable activities to do together. Here are a few of my favorites:

Mitten and Sock Tree — Cut out a Christmas tree-shaped piece of green felt. Attach the felt tree to a prominent wall in your home, Sunday school class, schoolroom, or Scout Troop meeting place. Ask the kids in your neighborhood or school to bring in new mittens and socks for the tree.

Before Christmas arrives, deliver the tree to a shelter for homeless or low-income children and adults. Include some large candy canes for a taste of the season.

Baskets of Love — Begin a yearly neighborhood project for the elderly or for a shut-in. Invite a group of neighborhood children over and divide them up into several groups. Have the groups make up Baskets of Love, and fill the baskets with greeting cards (Christmas, birthday, get-well, sympathy, etc.), postage stamps, address books, stickers, and confetti. Serve hot chocolate while the children put together the baskets for those who cannot shop for themselves. Deliver the baskets to a nursing home or to someone who is a shut-in to give them a way to share their love with others.

Holiday Hugs for Children

• **Lollipop Lane** — This easy-to-do craft keeps little guests happy and occupied while the adults visit together.

Lollipop Lane

Materials

> several 10-inch-round, 1-inch-thick disks of Styrofoam
> colored cellophane or colored plastic wrap
> several long dowel-rod sticks, about 1 inch in circumference
> colorful wide ribbon
> bread twisties

Directions

1. Secure rod in bottom of Styrofoam disk.
2. Wrap a large piece of cellophane or plastic wrap over Styrofoam disk.
3. With bread twistie, fasten cellophane where dowel rod and disk meet.
4. Tie over twistie with ribbon.

* These are perfect to decorate your front door with instead of a wreath. You can also make a whole bunch of them and line your sidewalks with cheery lollipops!

Menu

Christmas Cream
Peppermint Fudge
Handmade Caramels
Cinnamon Cocoa

Recipes to Nourish the Heart and Soul

Christmas Cream
Serves: 8

Ingredients

> 1 cup heavy cream
> 1 cup powdered sugar
> 2 teaspoons vanilla extract
> 1 quart (4 cups) perfectly clean snow

Directions

1. Whip cream until soft peaks form. Fold in sugar and vanilla.
2. Fold fresh, clean snow into cream mixture.
3. Eat immediately, or pack well-covered bowl outside your door in a snowbank and let chill until Christmas Cream has hardened.

Peppermint Fudge
Makes: 10-12

Ingredients

   1 1/2 cups sugar
   2/3 cup evaporated milk
   1/2 teaspoon salt
   2 cups mini marshmallows
   1 1/2 cups semi-sweet chocolate chips
   10 peppermint candies, crushed
   1/2 teaspoon peppermint extract

   1 teaspoon vanilla extract
butter

Directions

1. In a medium saucepan, mix sugar, milk, and salt over low heat.
2. Bring to a boil and simmer for approximately 4 minutes.
3. Remove from heat and add marshmallows, chocolate morsels, peppermint candies, and extracts.
4. Pour into a buttered 9-inch square glass and refrigerate until firm. Cut into 1-inch squares to serve.

Handmade Caramels
Makes: 4 dozen

Ingredients

   2 cups white corn syrup
   2 cups white sugar
   2 cups brown sugar
   1 pound butter
   2 cups cream

1 teaspoon salt
3 teaspoons vanilla

Directions
1. In a large pot, mix syrup, sugar, butter, and one cup of cream.
2. Cook over medium to medium-high heat for 15 minutes, then add second cup of cream and salt. Cook until 245 degrees or until candy reaches hard ball stage.
3. Add vanilla. Stir to combine.
4. Pour into two buttered jelly roll pans. When cooled, cut into squares. Wrap in wax paper, then wrap again in Christmas cloth or paper.

Cinnamon Cocoa
Serves: 14

Ingredients
6 cups unsweetened cocoa
2 cups malted milk powder
6 cups granulated sugar
4 tablespoons cinnamon

1 vanilla bean, split in half

Directions
1. Place all ingredients in a large bowl and blend together. Cover and let set for several days.
2. Spoon into gift jars. Include these instructions with your gift:
Mix 1/4 cup Cinnamon Cocoa Mix with 8-10 ounces of hot milk.

Packaging Panache

Serve the Christmas Cream in big red bowls. Sprinkle crushed peppermints and chocolate chips on top. Pack the peppermint fudge in a peppermint stick-decorated container. Attach candy canes to empty soup cans or glass jars with a hot glue gun. Leave the wrappers on and hot glue the candy canes side by side until the entire container is filled in. Tie a ribbon around the middle of the container and fill with peppermint fudge. (These also make great containers for holiday flowers!)

Kids' Crafts for Christmas

Transform an ordinary art project into a heavenly teaching time.
As you and your children make these crafts, discuss the Christmas
symbols—stars, bells, wreaths, and angels. See if the children know or can
figure out what each symbol stands for in relation to Jesus' birth. (For
example, stars symbolize the bright star that led the Wise Men to Jesus.
Wreaths are circles of evergreen that symbolize the gift of eternal life.
Angels symbolize the heavenly messengers who announced the birth of
Jesus.) Celebrate this Christmas with fun, meaning, and love.

Graham Cracker Nativity Scene

Materials
- graham crackers
- chocolate tube icing
- Chow Mein noodles
- 1 small bag pretzel sticks
- 1 chocolate bar

Directions
1. Using a table knife, carefully cut graham crackers into squares. Using chocolate tube icing as "glue," glue four crackers into an open square shape.
2. To make manger roof, tilt two cracker halves at an angle above open square and glue with icing. The triangular spaces above the cube can be filled in with diagonally-cut cracker halves.
3. Spread or squeeze icing onto one side of each pretzel stick and place sticks on manger walls.
4. To complete manger roof, break chocolate bar into two little sections and glue with icing to roof.
5. Fill in bottom of manger with Chow Mein noodles to resemble hay.

Pine Cone Snowmen

Materials
- graduated sizes of pine cones
- craft glue
- red and black felt
- scissors
- twigs

Directions

1. Cut off tops of pine cones. Put largest pine cone on bottom, medium-sized pine cone in middle, and smallest pine cone on top. Glue in place.
2. Cut out eyes, nose, and mouth from felt and glue on snowman's face.
3. Place twigs in sides of middle pine cone to create arms.
4. Top with a small top hat purchased from a craft store, or make your own from extra felt.

Edible Christmas Tree Place Cards

Materials

wax paper
knife
measuring cup
5 sugar cones
1 cup green icing
assorted sprinkles
small candies
red licorice strings
construction paper
star-shaped pattern or cookie cutter

Directions

1. Place sugar cones on wax paper.
2. Using a knife, cover each cone with green icing. Spread a generous amount on each cone to form peaks that look like branches of a Christmas tree.
3. Place sprinkles and candies all over cone to resemble ornaments. Wrap a red licorice string around your

tree for a garland.

4. Write names on small slips of construction paper and put in "branches" of tree.

3. Screw lid on very tightly. Turn upside down and watch it snow!

Christmas Snow Scenes

Materials

clean baby food jars or jelly jars (with lids)
white glitter
water-resistant heavy glue
small Christmas trees
water

Directions

1. Glue Christmas objects onto bottom of jar lid. Let dry overnight.

2. Fill jar with water until almost full. Add glitter.

Luminaries

Materials
  sand
  votive candles
  paper bags
  hole punch
  cloves or cinnamon
    sticks

Directions
  1. With hole punch,
     punch out a
     Christmas design
     on top portion
     of paper bag.
  2. Pour one cup
     of sand into
     bottom of bag.

Place candle in sand.
  3. Fill in around sand with
     cinnamon sticks and cloves
     for a holiday fragrance.

Toy Wreath

Materials
>   medium artificial green wreath
>   short pieces of florist wire
>   assortment of small toys
>   green florist tape
>   ribbon
>   wreath hanger

Directions
>   1. Wrap florist wire around small toys and affix to wreath. Tape off the ends of wire with green florist tape.
>   2. Twist a pretty Christmas ribbon in and out of toys and tie in a big bow on the bottom.
>   3. Hang toy wreath on your children's bedroom doors.

Angels We Have Heard on High

Materials
>   large roll of white butcher paper
>   pencils and markers
>   yarn
>   craft glue
>   netting

Directions
>   1. Unroll a piece of butcher paper about the length of a door.
>   2. Ask your child to carefully lie down on paper. Trace around his or her body using a marker.
>   3. Decorate the child's body outline to resemble a Christmas angel. Cut yarn and glue on for hair. Roll netting to resemble angel wings.
>   4. Use as a Christmas door badge.

A Christmas to Remember

MAKING MEMORIES FOR THOSE WHO ARE OLDER

Our hearts they hold all Christmas dear,
And earth seems sweet and heaven seems near.
—MARJORIE L.C. PICKENTHALL

Did you know that it's never too late to start a tradition or make a memory? Often the elderly are the very people who are most excited about experiencing something new at Christmas. While everyone else is reveling in the hustle and bustle the holidays bring, the lives of older people—especially those who live in nursing homes—remain much the same. They may only have a few decorations and a scheduled singing group or two to look forward to. During this time of year, it's important

to spend time with those living in nursing homes or those who cannot leave their homes. Spreading good cheer and a warm heart is the first order of business when ministering to the elderly. If you're headed to a nursing home, be sure to check with facility supervisors before planning your outing. Ask specifically about those who have no family around so you can give special attention to them.

Holiday Hugs for Adults

• **Pet Parade** — A pet parade is great fun for the residents of a senior center. Call the staff at a local facility and make arrangements with them first. It's a scientifically proven fact that animals lower people's blood pressure, and they are wonderful companions for those who cannot get out. Bring your own pets, borrow

your friends', or make arrangements to use some gentle critters from the local animal shelter. Bring along pretty Christmas ribbon and holiday bells to dress up the pets for the festive parade!

Holiday Hugs for Children

• **A Sunny Celebration** — Invite some young friends to join the pet parade. Ask several children to dress up their pets and accompany you to a retirement center or nursing home. Plan a Christmas sing-along, treats, and more for an afternoon sure to brighten many tomorrows for those who remember many a Christmas and most likely have some wonderful stories to share.

Menu
Pumpkin Cranberry Spice Bread
Lollipop Cookies
Herbal Teas

Recipes to Nourish the Heart and Soul

Pumpkin Cranberry Spice Bread
Makes: 2 loaves

Ingredients
> 2 1/4 cups all-purpose flour
> 1 tablespoon pumpkin pie spice
> 2 teaspoons cardamom
> 2 teaspoons baking powder
> 1 teaspoon nutmeg
> 1/2 teaspoon salt
> 2 eggs
> 1 cup granulated sugar
> 1 cup brown sugar
> 1 15-ounce can pure pumpkin

1/2 cup vegetable oil
1 cup fresh cranberries, chopped

Directions

1. Combine dry ingredients in a small bowl.
2. Combine eggs, sugars, pumpkin, and oil in a small bowl and beat until blended.
3. Add pumpkin mixture to flour mixture just until blended. Fold in cranberries. Spoon batter into two 9x5-inch pans that have been sprayed with cooking spray.
4. Bake in a 350 degree oven for 50-55 minutes or until a toothpick inserted comes out clean.
5. After breads have cooled, sprinkle with a powdered sugar and cinnamon mixture (1 cup powdered sugar mixed with 1 teaspoon cinnamon).

Lollipop Cookies

Makes: 2 dozen

Ingredients

1 package moist cake mix
3/4 cup apple juice
2 eggs
20-24 wooden popsicle sticks

Directions

1. Preheat oven to 375 degrees.
2. Place cake mix, juice, and eggs in a large bowl and mix on high speed for 2 minutes.
3. Drop rounded tablespoonfuls of dough 3 inches apart on a greased cookie sheet. Insert the wooden sticks 1 1/2 inches into edge of dough.
4. Bake for 8-11 minutes or until cookies are puffed and no indentations are left when touched gently. Cool. Remove from cookie sheet and cool further on a wire rack.
5. Decorate with frosting. Wrap finished lollipops with plastic wrap and then again with Christmas tissue paper. Secure bottom of tissue paper with a colorful ribbon.

Packaging Panache

Plant the lollipop flowers in a pretty basket. Fill the bottom of the basket with Styrofoam, then cover the Styrofoam with red and green grass or shredded Christmas paper. Insert the lollipop sticks into the Styrofoam and carry it around the nursing home. You or the children can invite the folks to pick a Christmas flower!

Carols and Bells

SPREADING GOOD CHEER THROUGH SONG

Heap the holly! Wreath the pine!
Train the dainty Christmas vine—
Let the breadth of fir and bay
Mingle on this festal day.
—HELEN CHASE

The thought of Christmas caroling inspires wonderfully warm memories of being all bundled up, ready to go forth and share the good news. Caroling is a delightful, old-fashioned way to share the spirit of the season with those around you. The unexpected treat of carolers showing up at the door is always a welcome surprise. Why not host your own caroling party? Invite a group of fun friends, suggest Dickens-style dress, and you'll be assured of a festive start to the holiday season. Who knows? You might even ignite the Christmas spirit in a former Scrooge!

Holiday Hugs for Adults

• **Caroling, Caroling** — Gather together some friends who love to sing and ring the bells of Christmas, and make it your mission to celebrate and orchestrate the season with style. The weekend after Thanksgiving, host a caroling party to get the season off to a cheerful start. Prepare some hors d'oeuvres, such as Glazed Peppered Pork Appetizers, and a batch of Christmas Popcorn. Play your favorite Christmas CDs and give Fragrant Trees as party favors.

To make the Fragrant Trees, purchase rosemary trees or petite cedars and plant them in terra cotta pots. Decorate the trees with Old-Fashioned Salt Dough Ornaments (see page 67) and display them around your home prior to the caroling party.

Give a tree to each guest as your party draws to a close. When the holidays are over, they can use the cut sprigs from a rosemary tree to make lemon-rosemary vinegar. It's a surefire way to add flair to those after-the-holidays, low-calorie suppers.

Holiday Hugs for Children

• **Merrily We Roll Along** — Fill a peppermint stick mailing tube with Christmas Popcorn and play a Christmas CD of the child's favorite music to fill the car or van with good cheer.

• **Terrific Trees** — Place a batch of Old-Fashioned Salt Dough Ornaments (see page 67) in a splatter-painted can, then top the can with petite Christmas cookie cutters and baking instructions. The baking dough will fill the house with the fragrance of the season. Children can also decorate Fragrant Trees—or their family tree—with these ornaments.

Menu

Glazed Peppered Pork Appetizers
Sugar and Cinnamon Star Tortilla
Crisps
Christmas Salsa and chips
Christmas Popcorn
Hot Chocolate, Hot Cider, Coffee,
and Tea

*Recipes to Nourish
the Heart and Soul*

Glazed Peppered Pork Appetizers
Serves: 8-10

Ingredients
    1 12-ounce jar orange
       marmalade, divided
    3 tablespoons orange juice

1 1/2 tablespoons butter, melted
1 tablespoon stone ground
    mustard
2 pork tenderloins
fresh cracked pepper
cooking spray

Directions
1. Combine 1/3 cup of marmalade
   with orange juice and butter;
   set aside.
2. Stir mustard into marmalade
   mixture; set aside.
3. Place tenderloins on a cooking-
   spray coated rack. Place rack in
   a broiler pan.
4. Brush tenderloins with marmalade mixture. Sprinkle with
   fresh cracked pepper and cover
   with foil.
5. Bake at 325 degrees for 15 minutes. Uncover and brush with
   marmalade mixture. Bake an
   additional 10 minutes or until

meat thermometer
reaches 160 degrees.

Sugar and Cinnamon Star Tortilla Crisps
Makes: 24 crisps

Ingredients
> 6 large tortillas
> 1/2 stick butter, melted
> 1/2 cup sugar
> 1 teaspoon cinnamon

Directions
1. Cut tortillas using a star-shaped cookie cutter.
2. Paint butter on tortillas with a pastry brush.
3. Combine sugar and cinnamon in a small bowl and sprinkle over butter-covered tortilla stars.
4. Bake at 350 degrees for 8-10 minutes

Christmas Salsa
Makes: 2 cups

Ingredients
> 6-8 Roma tomatoes, washed and chopped
> 1 medium yellow onion, peeled and chopped

3 jalapeno peppers, seeded
and chopped
2 tablespoons vinegar
2 tablespoons lime juice
1 tablespoon fresh garlic,
chopped
1 tablespoon oil
2 tablespoons cilantro,
chopped
12 flour tortillas
1/4 cup oil
1 tablespoon salt

Directions
1. Blend first 8 ingredients
together in a blender.
2. To make chips, cut shapes
out of tortillas with
Christmas cookie cutters.

Brush with a little oil and
sprinkle with salt. Bake at
400 degrees until crisp.

Christmas Popcorn
Serves: 8-10

Ingredients
1 cup butter or margarine
3/4 cup sugar
1 3-ounce package raspberry-
flavored Jell-O
3 tablespoons water
1 tablespoon light corn syrup
10 cups air-popped popcorn
2 cups honey-roasted peanuts

Directions
1. Combine first five ingredients
in a saucepan and bring to a

boil, stirring constantly.

2. Cook, stirring occasionally, until a candy thermometer reads 255 degrees.

3. Place popcorn and peanuts in a large bowl. Pour hot mixture over popcorn and stir until thoroughly coated. Spoon into a jelly roll pan.

4. Bake at 300 degrees for 10 minutes, stirring twice. Place on lightly greased aluminum foil; cool and break into pieces.

Packaging Panache

Purchase empty, quart-sized paint cans. (You can usually buy new ones at your local paint store.) Splatter-paint the outside of cans with red and green paints, then set aside to dry. When dry, stuff some colorful cellophane inside the can and wrap the dough for the Old-Fashioned Salt Dough Ornaments along with a few cookie cutters in the cellophane. Decorate the paint cans with festive holiday stickers. A sprig of greenery from a pine tree tops off your package with a fresh look. Include one with each Fragrant Tree gift.

White mailing tubes make great food containers for children's snacks. Wrap red electrical tape diagonally (spacing about two inches apart) down the mailing tube for a cute peppermint stick look. These make perfect holders for Christmas Popcorn!

The Twelve Doughs of Christmas

Start with a terrific sugar cookie dough, then let your imagination soar!

Super Delicious Sugar Cookies
Makes: 3 dozen

Ingredients
    2 cups shortening
    2 1/2 cups sugar
    2 teaspoons vanilla

3 eggs
1/4 cup milk
6 cups flour
4 1/2 teaspoons baking powder
3/4 teaspoon salt

Directions
1. Cream shortening, sugar, and vanilla. Add eggs to creamed mixture and mix well. Add milk and mix again.

2. Sift flour, baking powder, and salt. Add to creamed mixture and blend.
3. Add your favorite mix-in. (See suggestions below.)
4. Cover with plastic wrap and chill for 2 hours.
5. Bake in a 350 degree oven for 8-10 minutes or until golden brown.

12 Holiday Mix-Ins

- 1/2 cup cranberries and 1/2 cup white chocolate chips
- 1/2 cup chocolate chips and 1/2 cup crushed toffee bars
- 1/2 cup red cherries and 1/2 cup green cherries, chopped
- 1/2 cup fresh mint leaves, chopped
- 1/2 cup pistachios, chopped, and 1/4 cup fresh cranberries, chopped
- 1 cup red and green M&M's, combined
- 1/2 cup candied ginger, chopped
- 1 cup cinnamon Red Hots
- 1 cup mint chocolate chips
- 1/2 cup macadamia nuts, chopped, and 1/2 cup cranberries, chopped
- 1/2 cup candied orange rind, chopped, and 1/2 cup chocolate chips
- 1/8 cup cinnamon, 1/8 cup nutmeg, 1/8 cup powdered sugar*

* For this mix-in, roll dough out flat on a floured surface and sprinkle with swirls of cinnamon, nutmeg, and powdered sugar. Then roll dough up jelly roll fashion, slice, and bake.

Sharing the
Soul of Christmas

HOLIDAY HELPS FOR FAMILIES IN NEED

Practice tenderhearted mercy and kindness to others…
Most of all, let love guide your life.
—THE BOOK OF COLOSSIANS

*W*hen it's the time of year to be merry, hospitable, and full of
energy, families that are dealing with the strain of a serious illness often
feel left out. Life is very challenging for those who are making daily visits
to someone in the hospital or taking a loved one in for doctor visits
several times a week. This is an ideal time for friends and family to extend
open arms and offer helpful hands to ease a difficult situation. Offer to do
some shopping, baking, tree-trimming, or other errands to alleviate some

of the holiday pressures and add a spirit of warmth for the family members caring for their loved one.

And don't forget the person who is ill. During the busy holiday season, those who are sick often feel badly about not being able to physically help out. One wonderful gesture you can do is to suggest that when the family's Christmas cards begin arriving, put the ill family member in charge of praying for each family the card represents. That's a tremendous gift—one with lasting results!

Holiday Hugs for Adults

• **Lighted Path** — On a crisp December night, line your friend's driveway or walkway with festive and fragrant paper bag luminaries. This is a beautiful and bright way to welcome the season of the Christ child's birth. Gather up sand, votive candles, paper bags, and dried fruit potpourri. First, pour a cup of sand into each bag. Next, place candles in glass holders and secure the holders in the sand. Finish up by sprinkling around the candle with dried fruit potpourri. The glowing luminaries will provide a welcoming path home for families going through a trying holiday season.

Holiday Hugs for Children

• **Deck the Malls** — Offer to take the family's children Christmas shopping. Then bring them home with you and make Old-Fashioned Salt Dough

Ornaments or a Popcorn Wreath for delightful homemade gifts. Great for little people with little budgets!

Old-Fashioned Salt Dough Ornaments
Makes: 2 cups dough

Materials
>   1 1/4 cups flour
>   1/4 cup ground cloves + 1/4 cup cinnamon + 1/4 cup nutmeg (combined)
>   1 cup salt + 1 cup water (mixed together)

Directions
1. Mix all ingredients together.
2. Knead until dough is firm. If still sticky, sprinkle in some cinnamon.
3. Roll dough out on a cinnamon-sprinkled surface and cut out Christmas shapes with cookie cutters. Make a hole with a straw near the top of each cutout.
4. Bake at 300 degrees for 25-30 minutes.

* After these non-edible ornaments are cooled and decorated, thread a ribbon through the top hole and hang them on the tree.

Popcorn Wreath

Materials
>   1 Styrofoam wreath shape
>   green florist tape
>   8 cups popcorn, popped
>   1 package fresh cranberries
>   cinnamon sticks
>   whole cloves
>   glue
>   Mod Podge (available at craft stores)
>   ribbon

Directions
1. Wrap green florist tape around Styrofoam wreath.
2. Mix popped corn with 6 tablespoons of Mod Podge, stirring gently and thoroughly. Mixture will look milky white but will dry shiny. Spoon mixture around circumference of wreath.
3. Glue in cinnamon sticks and

whole cloves.
4. Tie ribbon around bottom part of wreath. Loop another piece of ribbon on top for easy hanging.

Menu
Ham with Marinade Mix
Cinnamon Shortbread
Pumpkin Butter
Orange Spice Tea

Recipes to Nourish the Heart and Soul

Ham Marinade Mix
Makes: 2 1/2 cups

Ingredients
1 cup Worcestershire sauce
1 cup pineapple juice
1/2 cup vinegar
1/2 cup brown sugar
1/4 cup Dijon mustard
6 cloves garlic

Directions
Combine ingredients in large jar, shaking well. Makes a delicious marinade for ham or beef; can also be used to baste meat during cooking.

Cinnamon Shortbread
Makes: 1 dozen wedges

Ingredients
2 sticks butter
1 cup brown sugar
1 tablespoon cinnamon
2 cups + 6 tablespoons cake flour
2 teaspoons apple juice

Directions
1. Preheat oven to 375 degrees. In a medium saucepan, melt butter over medium heat, stirring until lightly browned.
2. Remove from heat and quickly stir in brown sugar and flour.
3. Add 2 teaspoons apple juice and mix until dough is firm and crumbly.
4. Divide dough in half. Place each half in an 8-inch round cake pan and pat into a solid, even layer.

5. Using a fork, make perforated lines in top of dough, dividing it into 12 even wedges.
6. Bake for 20 minutes. Cool in pan on a rack for 15 minutes. Unmold and let cool completely. Cut into wedges along perforated lines.

Pumpkin Butter
Makes: 4 cups

Ingredients
  1 pound butter
  4 cups powdered sugar
  1 cup canned pumpkin
  2 teaspoons orange rind
  1/2 teaspoon pumpkin pie spice

Directions
  1. Mix butter and sugar until blended very smooth and soft.
  2. Add pumpkin, orange rind, and pumpkin spice. Mix to thoroughly combine.

Orange Spice Tea
Makes: 2 cups of mix

Ingredients
  1 cup orangeflavored Tang
  1 cup instant tea with lemon and sugar
  1/2 teaspoon cinnamon
  1/2 teaspoon cloves

Directions
  1. Mix ingredients and place in airtight container.
  2. To make one serving, stir 2 tablespoons Orange Spice Tea mix into 1 cup of boiling water.

Packaging Panache

Place gift items in decorated (but unlit!) luminaries. Add a few bits of the dried fruit potpourri to the bottom of the sack so that a fresh holiday fragrance will fill the air when it is opened. Tie closed with twine and accessorize with holly leaves. Place decorated Old-Fashioned Salt Dough Ornaments in bright red Chinese take-out containers. Adorn the tops with colorful bows and give them as tree-trimming gifts. Hang the Popcorn Wreath on the door of a child's room.

The Romance of the Season

Matrimony, mistletoe, and a lifetime of love

*Now join your hands, and with
your hands your hearts.*
—Shakespeare

Christmas is such a beautiful time of year for a wedding! Vibrant colors of the season, warm hearts, and the holiday spirit cannot help but make the special event even brighter. A wedding is truly one of the most important moments in a family's life—the day two hearts become one as a couple pledges a commitment to each other for life. Sharing your heart with the new family helps them to remember this occasion forever.

Holiday Hugs for Adults

• **Pretty as a Picture** — Collect Christmas photos from the bride's and groom's early years. Choose a variety of photos of each of them at approximately the same age, and frame the corresponding age shots in matching multiple-slot frames. Include a decorative Christmas picture hanger and velvet bows with the gift. This will make a delightful holiday display in the newlyweds' home for years to come.

• **Treasured Family Recipes** — Your family's tried-and-true holiday favorites are the perfect foods to share with a newly married couple. Create a Treasured Family Recipes book that gives them a head start on creating their own culinary traditions. The "old and new, borrowed and blue" concept can also work in the kitchen, the heart of the home. Tuck some Christmas activities that can become traditions (games, stories, creative ideas) throughout the pages of the recipe book. (For instance: *Before you open presents, read out loud the Christmas story from the Book of Luke.*)

Start your own tradition by sending the couple a recipe from a different food category along with a corresponding gift every year. For example, a cookie plate along with your favorite oatmeal-raisin bar recipe, or a pasta bowl with your best spaghetti sauce recipe taped inside. The couple will look forward to trying out a new and delicious recipe each year.

Holiday Hugs for Children

• **Let's Set Up House** — Let kids join in the fun of helping their newlywed friends set up house. Purchase two large stockings and some felt. Have the stockings professionally monogrammed for the couple, then let the kids do the rest. Show them how to cut the felt into shapes of items that represent the bride's favorites (flowers, basketball, horses) and the groom's favorites (football, chocolate, music) and glue these items to the stockings. Another fun idea is to purchase a small, fresh Christmas tree on its own stand. Children can decorate the tree with homemade ornaments and felt cut-outs. Deliver the decorated tree to the couple as a housewarming treat.

Menu
Assorted Meats and Cheeses
Grandmother Cabaniss' Dressing
Fresh Greens with Citrus Vinegar
Marshmallow Salad

*Recipes to Nourish
the Heart and Soul*

Grandmother Cabaniss' Dressing
Serves: 8-10

Ingredients
    2 cups celery, chopped
    1 stick butter
    4 cups cornbread
    2 cups biscuits
    3 eggs
    turkey stock or chicken stock
    salt and pepper to taste
    2 tablespoons (or to taste) fresh
        sage, chopped
    Crisco, melted for skillet

Directions

1. Put celery into a saucepan and add stick of butter. Saute until very tender.
2. Combine cornbread, biscuits, eggs, and seasonings in a large bowl. Stir together. Add enough stock to thoroughly dampen the mixture. (It should be the consistency of soft, uncooked cornbread, neither soupy nor dry. If too soupy, add more cornbread. If too dry, add more broth.)
3. Prepare a large iron skillet with Crisco oil. Pour dressing into hot skillet. Bake at 400 degrees for 45-50 minutes, or until golden brown.

Citrus Vinegar
Makes: 2 cups

Ingredients
1 large sprig fresh mint
1 long spiral lemon peel
1 long spiral orange peel
2 heaping tablespoons black peppercorns
2 cups white wine vinegar

Directions
Place first four ingredients in sterilized decorative bottles. Add vinegar and seal tightly. Set in a window for one month to let flavors blend, giving the jar a gentle shake every so often.

Marshmallow Salad
Serves: 8

Ingredients
1 pound large marshmallows
1 large can crushed pineapple, drained

1 cup sugar
3 eggs
1 tablespoon vinegar
1 cup almonds, chopped
1/2 pint whipping cream

Directions

1. Cut marshmallows into fourths and set aside.
2. Using an electric mixer, beat together sugar, vinegar, and eggs until thoroughly mixed. Place dressing mixture in top of a double-boiler and allow to thicken.
3. Add pineapple and almonds to marshmallows.
4. Stir hot custardlike dressing into marshmallow mixture. Cover and store in refrigerator overnight.
5. Before serving, beat whipping cream until soft peaks form. Stir into marshmallow salad.

* This salad is a great accompaniment to smoked turkey or ham.

Packaging Panache

Newlyweds creating a household together would enjoy a couple of festive Christmas serving plates. Place them in the center of two grapevine wreaths to showcase some delicious recipes. You can put the Treasured Family Recipe book on one plate and perhaps some tasty, freezable cookies on the other. If the couple is leaving for their honeymoon or headed out of town to visit family or friends, it is probably not the best time to provide them with food that needs to be eaten right away, like a big platter of dressing. A dish that freezes easily is a better choice.

Jingle Bells and Doggie Tails

Holiday Treats for Furry Friends

'Twas the night before Christmas,
when all through the house,
Not a creature was stirring,
not even a mouse.
—Clement Clarke Moore
"A Visit from St. Nicholas"

Families and pets go hand in hand, especially during the holidays. Furry

friends decked out in jingle bells offer a spirited touch to the home and

neighborhood. So before the days get too busy, make a plan for your pet.

Would Hot Diggity look better with a plaid bow or just a plain apple red

one? How about a new red flea collar for Louie the cat? You could even tie

Christmas bows to the tops of the rabbit cages. Pay attention to the "de-tails!"

Holiday Hugs for Adults

• **Pamper the Pets** — Be sure to include your pets in the holiday celebration. Smokey the cat loves the attention—especially a nice, warm lap to sit in while the family admires the Christmas tree. Muffin the dog loves the treats—a rawhide chew or some tasty Milk Bones. And a Christmas stocking filled with exotic seeds for S.J. the bird is a must!

Holiday Hugs for Children

• **Awesome Animals** — Puppy treats are great fun for kids to prepare. Bell-shaped Bowser Biscuits and tasty Holiday Hash are the perfect presents for the pets in your household.

Menu
Bowser Biscuits
Holiday Hash
Buddy's Bone Biscuits (for the family)

Bowser Biscuits (for the puppy)
Makes: 1 dozen

Ingredients
- 2 cups whole wheat flour
- 1/4 cup cornmeal
- 1/2 cup unbleached flour
- 1/4 cup pumpkin seeds
- 1 teaspoon salt
- 2 teaspoons salt
- 2 tablespoons butter
- 1/4 cup molasses
- 2 eggs, lightly beaten
- 1/4 cup apple juice

Directions

1. Mix all ingredients together in medium-sized bowl. Add more apple juice if dough is too firm.
2. Roll out dough to 1/2" thickness on a floured surface. Cut dough with your favorite cookie cutters and, of course, a bone-shaped cutter!
3. Place biscuits on a cookie sheet and bake at 350 degrees for 30 minutes, until toasted. If your pooch prefers harder biscuits, leave in oven with heat turned off for another hour.

Holiday Hash (for the puppy)
Makes: 3 cups

Ingredients

1 cup beef-flavored dog bones
1 cup small puppy beef jerky
1 cup puppy's favorite food

Directions

1. Combine all ingredients in a plastic container and shake.
2. Fill a small stocking with the "Holiday Hash," and tie the stocking closed with chewable rope. *Bark Appetit!*

Buddy's Bone Biscuits (for the family)
Makes: 2 dozen

Ingredients

3 cups all-purpose flour
1/2 cup dark brown sugar
1/2 teaspoon baking powder
1/2 teaspoon baking soda
1/3 cup honey
2/3 cup water

Directions

1. Preheat oven to 350 degrees.

2. In a large mixing bowl, combine flour, brown sugar, baking powder, and baking soda. Mix on low speed until all ingredients are combined.

3. Add honey and water and mix until combined.

4. Place dough on a lightly floured surface and roll to 1/2-inch thickness.

5. Using a bone-shaped cookie cutter, cut dough. Place bone shapes on a lightly greased cookie sheet.

6. Bake for 15-20 minutes, or until browned.

Packaging Panache

Write the pet's name on the top of a large stocking and fill it with Christmas treats. If your pet is already the proud owner of its own stocking, wrap the biscuits or another pet present in a brown paper bag that has been rubber-stamped with paw prints and deliver it displayed on a new Christmas-plaid puppy or kitty pillow.

Heartwarming Hints for Holiday Hospitality

Say "I love you" again and again throughout the holiday season with hundreds of fun and easy ideas for delicious recipes, festive crafts, and homemade treats.

Turn your home into a warm and welcoming winter wonderland. Simplify the big family feast. Share the reason for the season with your neighbors. Create fun family traditions that make children the center of the celebration. Give holiday love to those in need. You'll also find...

- 25 traditions to boost your Yuletide season
- 10 terrific tree trimming themes
- 12 sensational sugar cookie variations
- and much more

Share your heart, hearth, and home with warm holiday hospitality and recapture the spirit of an old-fashioned, homemade Christmas.

ISBN 0-7369-0339-9

9 780736 903394

$12.99

HARVEST HOUSE PUBLISHERS
Eugene, Oregon 97402

Gift